JAMES

BOOKS OF FAITH SERIES
Leader Session Guide

Mark Wickstrom

Augsburg Fortress
Minneapolis

JAMES
Leader Session Guide

Books of Faith Series
Book of Faith Adult Bible Studies

Copyright © 2010 Augsburg Fortress. All rights reserved. Except for brief quotations in critical articles or reviews, no part of this book may be reproduced in any manner without prior written permission from the publisher. For more information, visit: www.augsburgfortress.org/copyrights or write to: Permissions, Augsburg Fortress, Box 1209, Minneapolis, MN 55440-1209.

 Book of Faith is an initiative of the
Evangelical Lutheran Church in America
God's work. Our hands.

For more information about the Book of Faith initiative, go to www.bookoffaith.org.

References to *ELW* are from *Evangelical Lutheran Worship* (Augsburg Fortress, 2006).

Scripture quotations, unless otherwise marked, are from New Revised Standard Version Bible, copyright © 1989 Division of Christian Education of the National Council of Churches of Christ in the United States of America. Used by permission. All rights reserved.

Web site addresses are provided in this resource for your use. These listings do not represent an endorsement of the sites by Augsburg Fortress, nor do we vouch for their content for the life of this resource.

ISBN: 978-1-4514-0081-6

Writer: Mark Wickstrom
Cover and interior design: Spunk Design Machine, spkdm.com
Typesetting: Timothy W. Larson, Minneapolis, MN

The paper used in this publication meets the minimum requirements of American National Standard for Information Sciences—Permanence of Paper for Printed Library Materials, ANSI Z329.48-1984.

Manufactured in the U.S.A.
13 12 11 10   1 2 3 4 5 6 7 8 9 10

CONTENTS

Introduction		5
1	**What Is Wisdom?** *James 1:1-18*	9
2	**Wisdom: Faith and Action** *James 1:19—2:26*	19
3	**Wisdom: God's Sustaining Care for the World** *James 3–4*	27
4	**Wisdom: Healthy Habits that Sustain Christian Hope** *James 5:7-20*	34

Introduction

Book of Faith Adult Bible Studies

Welcome to the conversation! The Bible study resources you are using are created to support the bold vision of the Book of Faith initiative that calls "the whole church to become more fluent in the first language of faith, the language of Scripture, in order that we might live into our calling as a people renewed, enlivened, empowered, and sent by the Word."

Simply put, this initiative and these resources invite you to "Open Scripture. Join the Conversation."

We enter into this conversation based on the promise that exploring the Bible deeply with others opens us to God working in and through us. God's Word is life changing, church changing, and world changing. Lutheran approaches to Scripture provide a fruitful foundation for connecting Bible, life, and faith.

A Session Overview

Each session is divided into the following four key sections. The amount of time spent in each section may vary based on choices you make. The core Learner Session Guide is designed for 50 minutes. A session can be expanded to as much as 90 minutes by using the Bonus Activities that appear in the Leader Session Guide.

- **Gather (10-15 minutes)**
Time to check in, make introductions, review homework assignments, share an opening prayer, and use the Focus Activity to introduce learners to the Session Focus.

- **Open Scripture (10-15 minutes)**
The session Scripture text is read using a variety of methods and activities. Learners are asked to respond to a few general questions. As leader, you may want to capture initial thoughts or questions on paper for later review.

- **Join the Conversation (25-55 minutes)**
Learners explore the session Scripture text through core questions and activities that cover each of the four perspectives (see diagram on p. 6). The core Learner Session Guide material may be expanded through use of the Bonus Activities provided in the Leader Session Guide. Each session ends with a brief Wrap-up and prayer.

- **Extending the Conversation (5 minutes)**
Lists homework assignments, including next week's session Scripture text. The leader may choose one or more items to assign for all. Each session also includes additional Enrichment options and may include For Further Reading suggestions.

A Method to Guide the Conversation

Book of Faith Adult Bible Studies has three primary goals:

- To increase biblical fluency;
- To encourage and facilitate informed small group conversation based on God's Word; and
- To renew and empower us to carry out God's mission for the sake of the world.

To accomplish these goals, each session will explore one or more primary Bible texts from four different angles and contexts—historical, literary, Lutheran, and devotional. These particular ways of exploring a text are not new, but used in combination they provide a full understanding of and experience with the text.

Complementing this approach is a commitment to engaging participants in active, learner-orientated Bible conversations. The resources call for prepared leaders to facilitate learner discovery, discussion, and activity. Active learning and frequent engagement with Scripture will lead to greater biblical fluency and encourage active faith.

1 We begin by reading the Bible text and reflecting on its meaning. We ask questions and identify items that are unclear. We bring our unique background and experience to the Bible, and the Bible meets us where we are.

5 We return to where we started, but now we have explored and experienced the Bible text from four different dimensions. We are ready to move into the "for" dimension. We have opened Scripture and joined in conversation for a purpose. We consider the meaning of the text for faithful living. We wonder what God is calling us (individually and as communities of faith) to do. We consider how God's Word is calling us to do God's work in the world.

2* We seek to understand the world of the Bible and locate the setting of the text. We explore who may have written the text and why. We seek to understand the particular social and cultural contexts that influenced the content and the message. We wonder who the original audience may have been. We think about how these things "translate" to our world today.

Devotional Context

Historical Context

Lutheran Context

Literary Context

4 We consider the Lutheran principles that help ground our interpretation of the Bible text. We ask questions that bring those principles and unique Lutheran theological insights into conversation with the text. We discover how our Lutheran insights can ground and focus our understanding and shape our faithful response to the text.

3* We pay close attention to how the text is written. We notice what kind of literature it is and how this type of literature may function or may be used. We look at the characters, the story line, and the themes. We compare and contrast these with our own understanding and experience of life. In this interchange, we discover meaning.

* Sessions may begin with either Historical Context or Literary Context.

The diagram on p. 6 summarizes the general way this method is intended to work. A more detailed introduction to the method used in Book of Faith Adult Bible Studies is available in *Opening the Book of Faith* (Augsburg Fortress, 2008).

The Learner Session Guide

The Learner Session Guide content is built on the four sections (see p. 5). The content included in the main "Join the Conversation" section is considered to be the core material needed to explore the session Scripture text. Each session includes a Focus Image that is used as part of an activity or question somewhere within the core session. Other visuals (maps, charts, photographs, and illustrations) may be included to help enhance the learner's experience with the text and its key concepts.

The Leader Session Guide

For easy reference, the Leader Session Guide contains all the content included in the Learner Session Guide and more. The elements that are unique to the Leader Session Guide are the following:

- **Before You Begin**—Helpful tips to use as you prepare to lead the session.
- **Session Overview**—Contains detailed description of key themes and content covered in each of the four contexts (Historical, Literary, Lutheran, Devotional). Core questions and activities in the Learner Session Guide are intended to emerge directly from this Session Overview.
- **Key Definitions**—Key terms or concepts that appear in the Session Overview may be illustrated or defined.
- **Facilitator's Prayer**—To help the leader center on the session theme and leadership task.
- **Bonus Activities**—Optional activities included in each of the four sections of "Join the Conversation" used by the leader to expand the core session.
- **Tips**—A variety of helpful hints, instructions, or background content to aid leadership facilitation.
- **Looking Ahead**—Reminders to the leader about preparation for the upcoming session.

Leader and Learner

In Book of Faith Adult Bible Studies, the leader's primary task is facilitating small group conversation and activity. These conversations are built around structured learning tasks. What is a structured learning task? It is an open question or activity that engages learners with new content and the resources they need to respond. Underlying this structured dialog approach are three primary assumptions about adult learners:

- Adult learners bring with them varied experiences and the capability to do active learning tasks;
- Adult learners learn best when they are invited to be actively involved in learning; and
- Adults are more accountable and engaged when active learning tasks are used.

Simply put, the goal is fluency in the first language of faith, the language of Scripture. How does one become fluent in a new language, proficient in building houses, or skilled at hitting a baseball? By practicing and doing in a hands-on way. Book of Faith Adult Bible Studies provides the kind of hands-on Bible exploration that will produce Bible-fluent learners equipped to do God's work in the world.

Books of Faith Series

Book of Faith Adult Bible Studies includes several series and courses. This James unit is part of the Books of Faith Series, which is designed to explore key themes and texts in the books of the Bible. Each book of the Bible reveals a unique story or message of faith. Many core themes and story lines and characters are shared by several books, but each book in its own right is a book of faith. Exploring these books of faith in depth opens us to the variety and richness of God's written word for us.

James Unit Overview

The letter of James does not offer much information about who wrote it, when it was written, or who received it. What is clear is that the key to understanding and appreciating James is wisdom. *Wisdom* here means the creative gift of God that enables God's people to live and grow in responsible maturity. This advice for responsible, faithful behavior is scattered throughout James like pearls. Readers of James receive pearls of wisdom for living the life of faith.

Martin Luther called James an "epistle of straw" because its major focus is not Christ, the cross, and the resurrection. In other instances, however, Luther showed great appreciation for wisdom literature in the Bible. Many Christians over time have found comfort, strength, and power in the letter of James.

Session 1, What Is Wisdom? (James 1:1-18), describes how the power of God for living daily life is revealed in the collection of wisdom sayings in James.

Session 2, Wisdom: Faith and Action (James 1:19—2:26), explores how God's gift of wisdom binds together hearing and doing, faith and actions, in Christian life.

Session 3, Wisdom: God's Sustaining Care for the World (James 3-4), examines how wisdom's exhortations and commands represent the collective insights of the world and show God's sustaining care for the world.

Session 4, Wisdom: Healthy Habits that Sustain Christian Hope (James 5:7-20), looks at how prayer, praise, confession, and healing inspire hope for a community as it waits in the promise of our Lord's return.

SESSION ONE

James 1:1-18

Leader Session Guide

Focus Statement

The power of God for living daily life is revealed in the collection of sayings in the book of James.

Key Verse

If any of you is lacking in wisdom, ask God, who gives to all generously and ungrudgingly, and it will be given you. James 1:5

Focus Image

© Radius/SuperStock

What Is Wisdom?

Session Preparation

Before You Begin...

Take a few moments to think about wisdom. Write down your own definition of *wisdom*. Think about someone in your life who personifies wisdom. What characteristics does he or she display? What "pearls of wisdom" have been important in your life? Did someone give you these pearls, or did you discover them on your own? What role do you think God plays in acquiring wisdom? Is there a difference between wisdom and knowledge? What do you think of the following definitions?

- *Knowledge* is acquisition of information.
- *Wisdom* is applying knowledge in appropriate ways at the appropriate time.

Session Instructions

1. Read this Session Guide completely and highlight or underline any portions you wish to emphasize with the group. Note any Bonus Activities you wish to do.

2. If you plan to do any special activities, check to see what materials you'll need, if any.

3. Have extra Bibles on hand in case a member of the group forgets to bring one.

4. Keep in mind the conversational nature of Book of Faith adult Bible studies. Your role is to facilitate the conversation so that everyone has an opportunity to contribute to the discussion.

5. Mark the book of Proverbs in the Old Testament section of the Bible for easy access later in the session.

Session Overview

The main theme of James and the key to understanding and appreciating this letter is wisdom. *Wisdom* here means the creative gift of God that enables God's people to live and grow in responsible maturity. This advice for responsible, faithful behavior is scattered throughout James like "pearls" of wisdom. Though a number of New Testament books have examples of biblical wisdom, James is the only book in the New Testament primarily focused on this wisdom perspective. In this session we

SESSION ONE

will learn the source of wisdom, discover the role it is to play in a Christian's life, and discern the perspective that wisdom provides for all who acknowledge it.

Literary Context

James fits into a category of writing known as wisdom literature. This type of writing has a rich tradition in the Old Testament and appears in many places in the New Testament as well, including Jesus' teachings in the Sermon on the Mount (Matthew 5–7). A number of books in the Old Testament fit into the wisdom category. These include Proverbs, Job, and Ecclesiastes, to name a few. Wisdom can also be found in a number of psalms. The **Apocrypha** includes wisdom books, such as Sirach and Wisdom of Solomon.

Wisdom literature communicates advice and instructions from one in authority (a king, teacher, or parent), based on his or her experience of how to lead a successful life. In wisdom literature, wisdom is God's perfect gift. It belongs to God's goodness and purpose in creation, and it empowers all of creation, especially those who know the fear of the Lord (respecting and honoring God, living according to God's commands) as the beginning of wisdom.

In Proverbs, for example, wisdom is personified and speaks in the first person. "Woman Wisdom" calls and invites all to listen to her advice. Wisdom was present with God from the very beginning (see Proverbs 1:20-33; 8:1—9:6). This is the tradition that lies behind the letter of James.

Historical Context

Traditionally, the author of the book of James is identified as James the brother of Jesus (Mark 6:3), who led the Jerusalem church until his martyrdom just prior to the Jewish war of 66–70 C.E. (Galatians 1:19; Acts 15:13-21). However, many believe that James was written by someone who dedicated this religious work to a hero of the faith, a common ancient practice. The moral exhortation and references to testing, rich and poor in the assembly, doing business and making money, and laborers and harvest could fit with many times and settings.

The author of James does appear to come from the Jewish tradition. His reference to the "twelve tribes in the Dispersion" is a bit unclear. It may refer to the early Christian community and its Jewish roots, or to the people of Israel in general—and so to

---

Apocrypha:
This term is usually applied to the books that the Protestant Christian church considered useful but not to be included in the accepted canon, or list, of books in the Bible. Roman Catholic and Orthodox versions of the Bible include slightly different lists of apocryphal, also known as deuterocanonical, books.

Tip:
You may wish to have a Bible with Apocrypha available in class. *Lutheran Study Bible* includes a detailed chart of different Old Testament canons (see pages 28–29).

all Christians also. The names of the twelve tribes of Israel can be found in Numbers 1:20-43. If any in the group would like to know the names of the tribes, you could list them on chart paper or a whiteboard.

An interesting historical fact is that the book of James was one of seven books often disputed in the early church. In other words, not all early lists of accepted or authorized books included James. But eventually James became one of the 27 books that made up the New Testament canon.

Lutheran Context

Martin Luther had mixed feelings about the book of James. He believed that Jesus Christ, the cross, and the resurrection were at the heart of Scripture, but he did not see this reflected in James as clearly as in other New Testament books. For this reason, he sometimes referred to James as an "epistle of straw." Luther did include James in his translation of the Bible, however. He discussed it in prefaces to the New Testament and to the epistles and did not oppose people reading it.

Luther thought some New Testament books were more important because they so clearly communicated the gospel. This included Romans, Galatians, and John's Gospel, to name a few. Each had great substance and teaching about God's grace. For Luther, James did not compare in importance. Most modern folks are not familiar with the idea of putting the books of the Bible in any kind of hierarchy. Sometimes Lutherans talk of this hierarchy as a "canon within a canon." This means that all of Scripture is inspired and authoritative, but some passages bear the key message most clearly. Many Christians would look up or quote 2 Timothy 3:16 and assume that because all of Scripture was "inspired" by God, it is all of equal importance. Is that true for you or for your learners?

A key Lutheran principle for interpreting Scripture is "what shows forth Christ." You and your learners may at times find it hard to apply this principle directly while studying James. But as you hear God's wisdom in the letter, you might also think about Jesus as teacher, as one who embodies God's wisdom.

Devotional Context

In the Old Testament especially, wisdom is often linked to what we might call practical wisdom or common sense. Explore with the participants their own experiences with practical "pearls" of

SESSION ONE

wisdom that they have received from others or discovered on their own. In Old Testament wisdom, practical wisdom is linked directly to God and God's law. How are God's law and wisdom related to practical wisdom and laws we live by or are governed by?

You will also spend time considering the role of wisdom in the life of faith, as well as praying for the gift of wisdom. The important point to remember is that wisdom and law point to God's gifts that enable responsible maturity in the faith. But they do not replace the gospel. Many adults, including Christians, confuse living a good life with what it means to be Christian. This can lead to a sort of moralistic understanding of religion. But Christian faith puts Christ at the center. Our wisdom and "good work" flows from faith in Christ who has saved us by grace.

Facilitator's Prayer

Lord, your Scriptures have so much to teach us. Please set your Spirit free in our midst. Give the learners and me honesty to share openly the verses that confuse us. Encourage us with the verses that touch our hearts today, and grant us your wisdom to understand those verses that would add meaning to our walk with you. In Jesus' powerful name we pray. Amen.

Gather (10-15 minutes)

Check-in

Welcome each learner to the group. If there are new participants, or if group members are not familiar with one another, consider using name tags. If possible, refer to learners by name throughout the session. For reference, you might want to jot down names according to where they are seated. Invite each person to share a highlight or a lowlight from their past week. As leader, be prepared to go first to show the group how it is done.

Pray

Gracious God, thank you for revealing wisdom to us in the Bible. Empower us with wisdom to live faithfully in our daily lives. In Jesus' name we pray. Amen.

Tip:
Remind learners that it is okay to pass if they prefer not to share a highlight or lowlight.

SESSION ONE

Focus Activity

Write down as many wisdom quotes as you can in one minute. "An apple a day keeps the doctor away" would be an example. When you have completed your list, put a star by those sayings you have actually followed in your life. What do you observe?

 Tip:
You might note for the group that just being able to recite a wise saying doesn't mean we live by it. How many wise sayings actually influence our daily living? Might this be the beginning of wisdom?

Open Scripture (10-15 minutes)

Read the session Bible text yourself, or ask one or more volunteers to read the text aloud. Make sure that everyone has a Bible or can see one. Participants may follow along in their Bibles and underline key words or phrases, or they may simply listen with the three questions in the learner guide in mind.

Read James 1:1-18.
- How did you feel as you heard this text read?
- What words or phrases stand out the most to you?
- What questions do you have about this text?

Join the Conversation (25-55 minutes)

Literary Context

1. James is a letter that begins, like other letters in ancient times, by identifying the writer and recipient(s) and offering a salutation or greeting. The main theme of James and the key to understanding and appreciating this letter is wisdom. *Wisdom* here means the creative gift of God that enables God's people to live and grow in responsible maturity. This advice for responsible, faithful behavior is scattered throughout James like "pearls" of wisdom.

- Read James 1:1-4 and underline words and phrases indicating that James is a letter.
- Review James 1:1-18. Where does wisdom or the "word of truth" (1:18) come from, and how do we receive it?

2. Not only is wisdom the main theme and key to understanding and appreciating James, but also the letter

 Bonus Activity:
Have participants compare Proverbs 3:12 ("The LORD reproves the one he loves") to James 1:13 ("No one ... should say, 'I am being tempted by God'"). Have learners discuss their view on these two texts. How might the Lord discipline? Have they ever heard someone say that God gives people tests? Are these texts in conflict? If so, how might they be reconciled? If they are not in conflict, how do they complement one another?

Session 1: James 1:1-18

SESSION ONE

 Bonus Activity:
Invite learners to make a list of ways their faith has been tested. Ask them to choose one such time of testing and think about who or what caused the trial. If the testing is over, ask them to write down some insights they learned from going through that experience. Then invite them to read James 1:12. Has there been a crowning insight from the experience?

 Tip:
Wisdom in James comes from God as a gift (1:17). Believers are encouraged to ask for wisdom and strength to endure in prayer (1:5-6). The benefits of wisdom include insight, righteousness, justice, equity, shrewdness (Proverbs 1:1-9); fear (respect) for God and understanding (Proverbs 9:10; Psalm 111:10).

 Tip:
Some learners may be surprised by the idea that a person might write a letter using the name of a person more influential or recognizable (such as James, the brother of Jesus). Knowing the exact details of an author does not make a biblical book more or less trustworthy. The key is the book's message. They may also be surprised to find out that not all early Christians included James on the list of authoritative books of Scripture. This is a good example of how the church deliberates about matters to come to agreement or consensus.

 Bonus Activity:
James would become an important leader in the Jerusalem church. Invite learners to look up the following texts and make a list of important roles James is taking: Acts 15:13-21; Acts 21:17-25; Galatians 1:19; Galatians 2:8-10.

is made up of a specific type of writing called *wisdom literature*. This type of writing has a rich tradition in the Old Testament and appears in many places in the New Testament as well, including Jesus' teachings in the Sermon on the Mount (Matthew 5–7). Wisdom literature communicates advice and instructions from one in authority (a king, teacher, or parent), based on his or her experience of how to lead a successful life. In wisdom literature, wisdom is God's perfect gift. It belongs to God's goodness and purpose in creation, and it empowers all of creation, especially those who know the fear of the Lord (respecting and honoring God, living according to God's commands) as the beginning of wisdom. As you read through wisdom literature, wisdom sometimes speaks as "I" (in Proverbs 1:23-26, for example).

- What evidence do you find in James 1:1-18 that it is part of the wisdom literature in the Bible?
- Read Proverbs 1:1-9 and 20-33; Proverbs 9:10; and Psalm 111:10. List the benefits that are in store for the person who heeds wisdom.
- Read 1 Kings 3:5-14—Solomon's prayer for wisdom. How does this compare with James 1:5? King Solomon would have faced the temptations of wealth and power. Make a list of what James 1:12-16 says about temptation.

Historical Context

1. There is little detail in the letter of James to tell us who wrote it, when it was written, and who received it. Traditionally, the author is identified as James the brother of Jesus, who led the Jerusalem church until his martyrdom just prior to the Jewish war of 66–70 C.E. (Galatians 1:19, Acts 15:13-21). However, many believe that James was written by someone who dedicated this religious work to a hero of the faith, a common ancient practice. If this is the case, James may have been written as late as 130–140 C.E. The moral exhortation and references to testing, rich and poor in the assembly, doing business and making money, and laborers and harvest could fit with many times and settings. The address to "the twelve tribes in the Dispersion" is also unclear. It may refer to the early Christian community and its Jewish roots, or to the people of Israel in general—and so to all Christians also.

- What do you think about the fact that many things about the author, time, setting, and recipients of James are unclear? How does this affect the way you think about this letter?

2. Many writings and books were available to the early church. Early on, when Christians drew up lists of books that were

accepted, disputed, and rejected, James was one of seven books that were disputed. By the fourth century C.E., however, the 27 books in the New Testament, including James and the other "disputed" books, became *canon*—or the standard list—for Christians in the Greek and Latin traditions. Since that time, many Christians have drawn strength, comfort, and power from the letter of James.

- How does this affect the way you think about James?

Lutheran Context

1. Martin Luther had questions about James. He believed that Jesus Christ, the cross, and the resurrection were at the heart of Scripture, but he did not see this reflected in James as clearly as in other New Testament books. Luther did include James in his translation of the Bible, however. He discussed it in prefaces to the New Testament and to the epistles and did not oppose people reading it. More importantly, Luther's theology, teaching, and approach to Scripture demonstrate his appreciation and use of wisdom.

- Read Luther's explanation to the First Article of the Apostles' Creed in the Small Catechism. What does God do? What does God provide? How does this compare with James 1:5, 17-18?
- Lutheran teaching emphasizes grace—the undeserved gifts of God poured out on us through Jesus Christ. Review James 1:1-18 and underline words and phrases that tell about God's grace. How are grace and wisdom connected to each other?

2. Luther taught that some books in the Bible, such as the letters of Paul and the Gospel of John, are more important than other books because they more clearly show who Christ is and what Christ came to do. This criteria or principle is called "what shows forth Christ."

- What do you think about the idea that some books in the Bible are more important than others?
- On your own, list the books in the Bible that are most important to you. Compare your list with others in your group, and discuss how you made your choices.

Devotional Context

1. Look again at the Focus Image for this session. You've probably heard of the phrase "pearls of wisdom." What pearls of wisdom have been important in your life? Did someone "give" you those pearls, or did you discover them on your own?

Bonus Activity:
Ask volunteers to do some research on the topic of the creation of the New Testament canon. How long did the discussion about which books would be part of the accepted list go on? At what point was the matter mostly settled? What criteria was used to determine whether a book would make the list or not?

Tip:
Read the First Article and Explanation from *Luther's Small Catechism*. A number of versions exist, including one that can be found in *Evangelical Lutheran Worship* (p. 1160). God gives and preserves body and soul, as well as reason and all mental faculties. That would include wisdom. In addition, God gives physical gifts and protects from danger and evil. All is given, not because we have obeyed but out of God's divine goodness and mercy without any worthiness or merit on our part.

Bonus Activity:
If James had been dropped from the Bible, what do learners think might be missing from the New Testament? Have the group brainstorm some thoughts.

Tip:
Martin Luther's hierarchy on New Testament books was based on his belief that the message of the highest importance focused on Jesus, grace, and faith. Luther believed the books of greatest value were the Gospel of John, 1 John, Romans, Galatians, Ephesians, and 1 Peter. In his opinion, each of these books communicated the gospel message the most clearly.

Bonus Activity:
In Martin Luther's 1522 version of the New Testament, he put the books of Hebrews, James, Jude, and Revelation at the end as supplemental, rather than in their usual places. Had these books been eliminated from the New Testament, what important verses and/or ideas from each would no longer be considered Scripture? List some of those verses.

SESSION ONE

Tip:
You might consider how pearls of wisdom have been "strung together" in your own life. Be prepared to talk about your own pearls if the group needs your help to start talking.

Bonus Activity:
Have learners discuss whether they have ever had doubts concerning God and/or faith. Assure them that doubt is not the absence of faith, but is actually a sign of one who is engaged with God and belief. Even the disciples doubted.

Tip:
Some of the category headings you might consider: wisdom, warnings, Christian actions, healthy habits, rich and poor. You may discover others as you go through each of the chapters. This may be a helpful activity to repeat at the end of each session. In this way, as the themes of James reappear, their connectedness might make more sense.

2. James 1:2 calls us to consider trials or times of testing as "nothing but joy." Tell about someone who faced a difficult time with joy. How was joy possible during this time?

3. James tells us to ask God for wisdom. We are to ask in faith, not doubt, which is "like a wave of the sea, driven and tossed by the wind" (1:6-8).
- Draw or describe how you would picture doubt, then do the same for faith. What similarities and differences do you see between doubt and faith?

4. Write or say a prayer asking and expecting God to give you the gift of wisdom.

Wrap-up

1. Ask learners: What did you learn in this session that was new or surprising? How do you see James or your own faith in a different way?

2. If there are any questions to explore further, write them on chart paper or a whiteboard. Ask for volunteers to do further research to share with the group at the next session.

3. Explain and assign any homework for the coming week.

Pray

God of wisdom, thank you for showering us with every good gift. When we face difficult times, give us the courage to change the things we can change and to let go of things we cannot control. When we have doubts, be our anchor and strengthen our faith. Give us the gift of wisdom to live and grow in your grace. In Jesus' name we pray. Amen.

Extending the Conversation (5 minutes)

Homework

1. Read the text for the next session: James 1:19—2:26.

2. Find three passages in James 1:1-18 that really speak to you. Write each one on an index card and carry the cards with you. After every meal, take out one of the cards and read it.

3. Check out the Book of Faith Web site at www.bookoffaith.org and consider starting or joining a conversation on the book of James.

4. Think about a trial or difficulty you are experiencing in your life right now. Pray for God's wisdom in this situation each day for the next week, expecting God to give generously.

5. As you review this week's session text or read the text for the next session, consider using the following questions to guide you:
- Which verse or verses causes me some concern?
- Which verse or thought enlightens me right now?
- Which verse or thought encourages me right now?

Be prepared to share your responses with the group, if you wish to volunteer.

Enrichment

1. Do some additional research on the meaning of *wisdom* in the Bible. For example, read about wisdom literature in a study Bible, look at an introduction to the book of Proverbs, or do an online search on the term "biblical wisdom." Prepare a brief report to share with the group.

2. If you are looking for insights on how to deal with trials related to addictions, check out a 12-step program such as Alcoholics Anonymous or Gamblers Anonymous. Check local listings for groups meeting near you. If you are looking for insights on how to deal with a loved one who has an addiction, check out Alanon or a treatment center near you.

3. Listen to a recording of the song "Turn, Turn, Turn (To Everything There Is a Season)" (Book of Ecclesiastes/Pete Seeger, Columbia Records, 1965) by The Byrds. The song is based on the wisdom literature in Ecclesiastes 3:1-8. What life experiences does it highlight? How many does it mention? They are presented in random fashion, probably because life can happen in just such random ways. Which of these experiences have you encountered in your life?

For Further Reading

First and Second Peter, James, and Jude by Pheme Perkins. Interpretation, a Bible Commentary for Teaching and Preaching (Louisville, Ky.: Westminster John Knox Press, 1995).

Tip:
There are 28 different life experiences mentioned. Consider doing this activity in class.

SESSION ONE

> Available at www.augsburgfortress.org/store:
>
> *James, 1 Peter, 2 Peter, and Jude* by John H. Elliott and R. A. Martin. Augsburg Commentary on the New Testament (Minneapolis: Augsburg Books, 1982).
>
> *Lutheran Study Bible* (Minneapolis: Augsburg Fortress, 2009).

Looking Ahead

1. Read the text for the next session: James 1:19—2:26.

2. Read through the Leader Guide for Session 2 and decide which portions you want to cover in next week's session.

3. Make a checklist of materials you will need to do any of the activities, including Bonus Activities.

4. Pray for members of your group during the week.

SESSION TWO

James 1:19—2:26

> Leader Session Guide

Focus Statement
God's gift of wisdom binds together hearing and doing, faith and actions, in Christian life.

Key Verse
But be doers of the word, and not merely hearers who deceive themselves.
James 1:22

Focus Image

In Christian life, faith and actions are joined together like inhaling and exhaling.
© Flirt / SuperStock

Wisdom: Faith and Action

Session Preparation

Before You Begin . . .

This session uses the natural relationship between breathing in and out to illustrate the relationship between faith and works, so take a few moments to do some centered breathing. Sit in a chair with your back straight and your feet flat on the floor. Close your eyes. Place your hands palms up in your lap. Now, take a deep breath in through your nose. Hold your breath and count to three, then exhale slowly through your mouth. Repeat this exercise several times until you feel relaxed. Then listen to your breathing. Pay attention to your breathing pace, and try to make it comfortably slow and relaxed.

Session Instructions

1. Read this Leader Session Guide completely and highlight or underline any portions you wish to emphasize with the group. Note any Bonus Activities you wish to do.

2. If you plan to do any special activities, check to see what materials you'll need, if any.

3. Have extra Bibles on hand in case a group member forgets to bring one.

4. Keep in mind the conversational nature of Book of Faith adult Bible studies. Your role is to facilitate the conversation so that everyone has an opportunity to contribute to the discussion.

Session Overview

This session seeks to illustrate the natural relationship between faith and actions, hearing and doing, in Christian life. The premise is that faith sets actions in motion. Faith and actions, hearing and doing, are bound together like inhaling and exhaling when we breathe.

LITERARY CONTEXT

James 1:19 encourages the reader to be "quick to listen." Our ability to listen is affected by several factors, including the subject matter (Is it interesting to the listener? Is it simple to understand or complex? Does it require special knowledge or a

SESSION TWO

certain vocabulary?), speaker (Is the presenter competent? Does the speaker use various tones of voice? Does the presenter's appearance cause any distractions?), presentation (Is the information shared with visual illustrations? Are there examples from real life?), and environment (Is the room conducive for listening? Are there distractions?).

This session would be an ideal time to discuss the value of listening, both in general and as good advice for the group's time together. Why is it wise to "be quick to listen, slow to speak"? How will good listening help your group's discussions?

The focus of this session is on the relationship between hearing and doing, faith and actions. While we often see these as opposites, James sees them as parts of one whole, making up Christian life. They are bound together as one, like inhaling and exhaling as we breathe. Invite participants to discuss how faith affects their actions and how actions affect their faith.

Also note what James is not saying. Faith and actions make up the Christian life, but they are not the basis for our salvation. We are saved because of Christ's death and resurrection, not because of what we do or don't do. This critical point appears in the Lutheran Context for this session.

Historical Context

In ancient Mediterranean society, men could own property and make a living, but women and children were not allowed to do these things. This meant that women and children depended on the men in their lives to provide for their needs. Widows, orphans, and those who were poor were pushed to the margins of society and struggled to survive.

Throughout the Bible, God shows concern for widows, orphans, and those who are poor. God's people are called to care for these groups as well. In the book of Ruth, the land owner Boaz harvests his crops, but the grain that falls off the wagon or into the corners of the field is not picked up. It is left for less fortunate citizens, like Ruth, to glean or gather (Ruth 2:2). Later on, Boaz purposefully leaves stalks of grain for Ruth as an additional act of generosity (Ruth 2:15-16). In Matthew 25:35-40, Jesus tells the righteous that any time they take care of the physical needs of others, they are actually ministering to Jesus.

James 1:19—2:26 picks up on this care and concern for those who are marginalized and points out that words are not enough when someone needs food or clothing.

Lutheran Context

Martin Luther was a monk and a priest during the Middle Ages. This was a time when the church emphasized good works or actions as the way to salvation. In fact, the church granted **indulgences** in return for good works and prayers. Indulgences were believed to "save" people by providing full or partial remission of the punishment due for sin. They could even be purchased for a price paid to the church.

In spite of the fact that the church was practicing indulgences, Luther came to the conclusion that salvation could not be purchased. Rather, it was a free gift of God (Ephesians 2:8-9). This gift of grace was made possible by the life, death, and resurrection of Jesus Christ.

Luther believed that because of the grace received through Christ, actions or good works would surely follow. This makes actions natural parts of life in faith, not requirements for salvation.

In baptism we receive new life and are set free to love and care for the neighbor. Luther understood this calling as our vocation, and he believed that vocation could be carried out at home, at work, and in the community, as well as in the church.

Devotional Context

First-century customs and beliefs dictated that the more powerful a person was, the better the seat he or she should have at meals and in worship. And yet, James 2:1-13 warns readers against any form of favoritism or discrimination because it goes against God's command to love the neighbor.

We are often tempted to judge others based on how they look, act, or believe, and to withhold love and mercy from those we do not fully understand or find loveable. In the face of this, James suggests that all people have equal value and importance in God's kingdom.

As you come to the end of the session, be sure to give participants time to reflect on the relationship between faith and actions in their lives.

> **? Indulgences:**
> Full or partial reduction in the punishment for sin. During the Middle Ages, the church sold indulgences, a practice Martin Luther condemned.

SESSION TWO

Facilitator's Prayer

Gracious God, thank you for saving me from sin and giving me new life. Let my thanks overflow in love and care for my neighbor and for the members of this group. Be with us as we explore the connection between faith and actions. In Jesus' name we pray. Amen.

Gather (10-15 minutes)

Check-in

Welcome each learner to the session. If there are new participants, or if group members are not familiar with one another, consider using name tags. If possible, refer to learners by name throughout the session. Invite each person to share a highlight or a lowlight from the past week. As leader, be prepared to go first to show the group how it is done.

 Tip: Remind learners that it is okay to pass if they prefer not to share a highlight or lowlight.

Pray

Lord, thank you for the gift of wisdom that joins together faith and actions in our new life in Christ. Strengthen our faith and empower our actions for the sake of your kingdom. In Jesus' name we pray. Amen.

Focus Activity

Reflect on the Focus Image. Life is only sustained if we breathe in *and* breathe out. What do you think of the idea that faith and actions are like breathing? If you agree with this idea, which one is breathing in, and which one is breathing out? Why?

 Tip: Before discussing the questions, give participants the opportunity to do some centered breathing. Have them get started by sitting in their chairs with their backs straight, their feet flat on the floor, their hands resting in their laps with their palms up, and their eyes closed. Each person should then take a deep breath in through the nose, hold that breath, and, after you count to three, exhale slowly through the mouth. Repeat this exercise a few times until participants feel relaxed. Encourage them to listen to their breathing and try to make their breathing pace comfortably slow and relaxed.

Open Scripture (10-15 minutes)

Ask for volunteers from the group—one to read James 1:19-27, one to read 2:1-13, and one to read 2:14-26.

Provide paper and markers for participants to write down words, draw images, or doodle as they listen to a reading of the text.

Read James 1:19—2:26.
- What words in this text stand out to you?
- What feelings do you have as you hear this text read?
- What questions do you have?

SESSION TWO

Join the Conversation (25-55 minutes)

Literary Context

1. James says, "Be quick to listen, slow to speak, slow to anger" (1:19). Compare this to James 2:15-17. How might we become more aware of the needs of others?

2. Throughout James, wisdom is the supreme mark of God's gift of creation. Faith is trusting in the power of that gift to help us weather the storms of life and grow to a maturity expressed in "religion that is pure"—caring for those who are poor and in need (1:5-15, 27). In this way, wisdom binds together faith and works, hearing and doing. This unity is as essential as that of body and spirit (2:26).

- Review James 2:14-26 on faith and works, one of the longest sections in this brief letter. List reasons why, according to James, it is crucial to see that hearing and doing, and faith and works, are bound together as parts of one action, like breathing.

Historical Context

1. Ancient Mediterranean society marginalized widows, orphans, and those who were poor, and they struggled for survival. Throughout the Bible, however, God shows concern for widows, orphans, and those who are poor, and believers are called to care for these groups.

- Review the session Scripture text and identify the passages that demonstrate this biblical concern for widows, orphans, and those who are poor, and the call to care for them.

2. In the Middle Ages, those in monasteries were obligated to help anyone who asked for food or shelter. Some of the earliest hospitals in Europe and America were established by Christians. Still today, many hospitals, long-term care facilities, and organizations that assist with other needs have a Christian background or mission.

- Based on James 1:19—2:26, how would you explain this care and concern for people in need?

Lutheran Context

1. In Martin Luther's time, the church emphasized works or actions as the way to earn salvation. In contrast to this, Luther's insight on justification by grace through faith put the focus on what God has already accomplished, rather than on what we do. Salvation, Luther said, is not something we earn by what we do. It is a gracious gift of God that comes to us through the suffering, death, and resurrection of Jesus Christ.

Bonus Activity:
Invite participants to list or act out some characteristics of a good listener. These characteristics might include looking at the speaker, nodding affirmatively, staying alert, smiling, asking for clarification, taking notes, suggesting examples from personal experience, and repeating or rephrasing what is said.

Tip:
Use chart paper or a whiteboard to write down the group's responses.

Bonus Activity:
Challenge your group to name some other things that are joined together as one, like faith and works, hearing and doing.

Tip:
The point in this section is that God cares for people in need and calls us to do the same.

Bonus Activity:
Encourage participants to identify some groups who may be marginalized or cast aside in today's society.

Tip:
Be aware that some participants may feel that, for various reasons, they have been marginalized by today's society.

Bonus Activity:
Discuss how your congregation reaches out to people in need.

Bonus Activity:
Provide a variety of art materials. Invite participants to create something that reminds them that salvation is a gift from God.

SESSION TWO

Tip:
Many people have the impression that Martin Luther's questions about James were based on the discussion of faith and works. Keep the Lutheran Context from Session 1 in mind here. Luther's questions about James arose because he did not see Jesus Christ, the cross, and the resurrection reflected in this letter as clearly as in other New Testament books.

Tip:
Before the session, think about the roles you play in carrying out your vocation, and be ready to share an example of how you serve others in one of those roles.

Bonus Activity:
Luther taught that we also serve God through our vocations. Encourage participants to identify how they serve God as employers, employees, parents, siblings, children, friends, neighbors, and so on.

Tip:
Have participants form smaller groups of two or three to discuss the questions.

Tip:
Provide paper and markers for participants to use.

Bonus Activity:
Invite participants to tell about someone whose faith and actions are intertwined.

Tip:
As in Session 1, some of the category headings you might consider are wisdom, warnings, Christian actions, healthy habits, rich and poor.

- Review the session Scripture text and identify why it is important to have faith and works together. Discuss whether James contradicts what Luther says about how we are saved.

2. In Baptism we are given new life, which sets us free to be what God intended all along. We are called to love and care for the neighbor. Luther referred to this baptismal calling as our *vocation*. We can carry out our vocation to serve others in many ways—as employers, employees, parents, siblings, children, friends, neighbors, and so on.

- List the ways you currently carry out your vocation. Choose one item from your list and tell how you serve others in that vocational role.
- In our vocations, as in faith, hearing and doing come together. Give an example of how hearing and doing are essential to one of the ways you carry out your vocation.

Devotional Context

1. In the first century, common belief and practice dictated that the more powerful a person was considered, the better the seats he or she should be given at a meal or in worship. The practice of favoritism is condemned in James 2:1-13. James suggests that in God's kingdom, all people are of equal value and importance.

- Why do you suppose people who have power or wealth are often treated better than others? What prevents people from treating everyone the same?
- What forms of favoritism exist in your community, church, or workplace? Brainstorm a list of ways to deal with these forms of favoritism.

2. Consider these questions: How has faith affected what you do to serve and care for others? How has serving and caring for others affected your faith? Has faith ever strengthened your serving and caring? Has serving and caring ever strengthened your faith? Then draw or describe the relationship between faith and actions in your life.

Wrap-up

1. Ask the learners: What did you learn in this session that was new or surprising? How do you see James or your own faith in a different way?

2. If there are any questions to explore further, write them on chart paper or a whiteboard. Ask for volunteers to do further research to share with the group at the next session.

3. Explain and assign any homework for the coming week.

Pray

Lord of all wisdom, thank you for saving us through your gracious actions and setting us free to follow your call to serve and care for others. Strengthen us to follow this call at home, work, and church, and with neighbors close by and far away. In Jesus' name we pray. Amen.

Extending the Conversation (5 minutes)

Homework

1. Read the next session's Scripture text: James 3-4.

2. With one or two other people, or with your entire group, brainstorm a list of people you would like to assist in some way. These might be people in your congregation or people in need in the surrounding community. Choose an individual or group on your list and make arrangements to visit with them. Take some time to listen to the person or group to find out what forms of assistance would be needed and appreciated. You might decide to do a project once a week, once a month, or once a quarter.

3. Create a video that shows how not to treat visitors when they come to worship at your church. Have fun exaggerating what not to do. Consider when and where you might show this video to others in the congregation.

Enrichment

1. Watch a movie that captures the negative effects of favoritism, such as *Philadelphia* (Sony Pictures, 1993), *The Color Purple* (Amblin Entertainment, 1985), *Mississippi Burning* (MGM, 1988), or *A Time to Kill* (Regency Enterprises, 1996). Or choose a movie that captures the power of treating people with equality, such as *Joshua* (Lions Gate, 2002), *Driving Miss Daisy* (The Zanuck Company, 1989), or *Remember the Titans* (Walt Disney Video, 2000).

SESSION TWO

2. During the week, journal about how your faith and actions are intertwined.

3. Write or say a prayer asking God for wisdom in living out your vocation to serve others.

For Further Reading

Fully Human, Fully Alive: A New Life through a New Vision by John Powell, S.J. (Argus Communication, 1976).

Reaching Out: The Three Movements of the Spiritual Life by Henri J. M. Nouwen (New York: Doubleday, 1975).

Looking Ahead

1. Read the text for the next session: James 3–4.

2. Read through the Leader Guide for Session 3 and decide which portions you want to cover in next week's session.

3. Make a checklist of materials you will need to do any of the activities, including Bonus Activities.

SESSION THREE

James 3–4

Leader Session Guide

Focus Statement
Wisdom's exhortations and commands represent the collective insights of the world. They are signs of God's sustaining care for the world.

Key Verse
The wisdom from above is first pure, then peaceable, gentle, willing to yield, full of mercy and good fruits, without a trace of partiality or hypocrisy. James 3:17

Focus Image

© Martin Heitner / SuperStock

Wisdom: God's Sustaining Care for the World

Session Preparation

Before You Begin . . .

Think about what it would be like to drive without any road signs, speed limits, and other "rules of the road."

Session Instructions

1. Read this Leader Session Guide completely and highlight or underline any portions you wish to emphasize with the group. Note any Bonus Activities you wish to do.

2. If you plan to do any special activities, check to see what materials you'll need, if any.

3. Have extra Bibles on hand in case a group member forgets to bring one.

4. Keep in mind that your role is to facilitate the conversation so that everyone has an opportunity to contribute to the discussion.

Session Overview

It is easy for us to see how laws and rules restrict our freedom to do whatever we want. The challenge in this session is to see the goodness of God's law in promoting and sustaining life. The gift of wisdom shows God's sustaining care for all of creation.

Literary Context

Throughout the Bible, God's law is described as good, and it is seen as something that promotes and sustains life. In keeping with this, James is confident in the belief that wisdom is a gift of God and a major sign of God's grace and sustaining care for the world. In a society that values independence and freedom, this may be difficult to understand, but examples can help. A loving parent will tell a child, "Look both ways before you cross the street." To the child this sounds like a restriction, but this restriction preserves the child's life and health. A society sets up traffic laws that limit what is allowed, but these limitations make roads safer for drivers and pedestrians. God's law says, "You shall not lie about your neighbor." This law restricts and limits what we can do, but it also encourages peace among us and our neighbors and promotes life in the community.

Session 3: James 3–4   27

SESSION THREE

> **? Metaphors:**
> Images used to illustrate a point or idea by comparing one thing to another.

In the Literary Context, we also look at the use of **metaphors** in the session Scripture text. James uses images of the bit in a horse's mouth and the rudder on a ship to illustrate how a small thing—like a person's tongue or speech—can have a large effect. The writer wants readers to be aware that words can build up, but they can also tear down and destroy people, relationships, and communities. Here again, James passes along wisdom to sustain and promote life.

HISTORICAL CONTEXT

When we explore the historical context of a Scripture text, we often consider the original audience. Early Christians would have been the first to read the letter of James. The letter does not pinpoint the exact location and time of these original readers. However, early Christians may have struggled to identify how they should relate to laws and rules of the world they lived in. Did the commands and rules of the secular world have any connection to their Christian witness?

James sees no conflict between the world's collective wisdom, which inspires life-sustaining and life-promoting laws and rules, and God's grace. Instead, the wisdom of the world is simply one sign of God's love and care for the world. It is a gift given by God to all creation.

LUTHERAN CONTEXT

With his teachings on the Ten Commandments and on the two kingdoms, Martin Luther made significant contributions to theological thinking about wisdom and God's sustaining care for the world. His explanations of the commandments begin with, "We are to fear and love God . . ." (*Luther's Small Catechism*, Augsburg Fortress, 2008), hearkening back to Proverbs 1:7 and other wisdom literature in the Bible. Each explanation moves beyond prohibited behavior to promote words and actions that show God's love and mercy in the world.

Luther's doctrine of the two kingdoms shows his thinking on how God works through wisdom and law. Humans live in two kingdoms simultaneously, Luther said: the kingdom on the right and the kingdom on the left. In the kingdom on the right, God works through the gospel, helping us understand that justification comes only through God's mercy and grace in Jesus' death and resurrection. In the kingdom on the left, which is the kingdom of this world or the world of creation, God works through wisdom, law, and commands, preserving and sustaining life. In this kingdom, God also gives us wisdom and human insights to care for the neighbor and imagine and develop better ways of living.

Confusion arises when we try to apply wisdom and law to the kingdom on the right and attempt to earn salvation through doing good works and following the law. Luther's two kingdoms doctrine helps to set us straight here. While wisdom and law serve to preserve and sustain life in the kingdom of this world, they are not the operating principles for the kingdom on the right, where God rules with mercy and grace through the cross of Jesus Christ.

Devotional Context

The Devotional Context is a place for participants to begin or continue to sort out the meaning of the session Scripture text as individuals, a group, a community of faith, and so on. They will reflect on God's saving work in the death and resurrection of Jesus Christ and respond to a very open-ended question about what challenged or delighted them in this session.

Facilitator's Prayer

Wise and holy God, give me the gift of wisdom. Lead me and help me to lead this group. Guide me and help me to guide the group's discussion. Bless me and help me to be a blessing to each group member. In Jesus' name I pray. Amen.

Gather (10-15 minutes)

Check-in

Welcome each learner to the session. If there are new participants, or if group members are not familiar with one another, consider using name tags. If possible, refer to learners by name throughout the session. Invite each person to share a highlight or a lowlight from the past week.

 Tip: Again, remind learners that it is okay to pass if they prefer not to share a highlight or lowlight.

Pray

Loving God, we easily overlook the goodness of your law and the gift of your wisdom. Help us to see how your law promotes and sustains life, and how wisdom shows your sustaining care for all of creation. Be with us as we study and learn from your Word and from one another. Amen.

SESSION THREE

 Tip:
Use chart paper or a whiteboard to write down signs of God's wisdom in the world. Consider adding items to this list throughout the session.

Focus Activity

Take a look at the Focus Image. How do you feel about road signs, speed limits, and other "rules of the road"? Where do you find "signs" of God's wisdom in the world?

Open Scripture (10-15 minutes)

In pairs or trios, have participants take turns reading the text to each other and listening carefully as the text is read.

Encourage participants to listen for the imagery in the text as it is read. Provide some time for them to sketch out one or two images and share these "word pictures" with the group.

Read James 3–4.
- What words in this text stand out to you?
- How do you feel as you listen to this reading?
- What questions does this text raise for you?

Join the Conversation (25-55 minutes)

Literary Context

1. In its 108 verses, the book of James contains more than 50 examples of exhortations or commands. James sees these exhortations and commands in a positive way, as the collective insights of human wisdom. Given by God in creation, this wisdom is a major sign of God's grace (James 1:17-18).

Read the following texts and note how exhortations and commands are described as gifts from God that promote and sustain life.
- Deuteronomy 4:1-14
- Psalm 1
- Proverbs 1:1-7; 8:1-21
- Matthew 7:24-27
- Romans 13:8-10
- 1 Corinthians 10:23

Tip:
Consider having participants work in pairs. Assign a text for each pair to read, discuss, and report back to the larger group.

SESSION THREE

2. Writers often use metaphors to illustrate a point or idea. Metaphors are images used to compare one thing to another. For example, in James 3:1-3, the writer uses the metaphor of a bridle and horse to illustrate how a small thing—like a person's tongue or speech—can have a large effect.

- Read James 3:1-12 and list other metaphors used by the writer. How do these images apply to the tongue, words, and speech?

Historical Context

Early Christians may have struggled to identify how the wisdom of this world (the sum total of all the commands and rules of the secular world) might be connected to the Christian witness to God's love and mercy as known in the life, death, and resurrection of Christ. In James, however, there is no conflict between the world's collective wisdom and God's grace. Instead, the wisdom of the world is simply one sign of God's love and care for the world. It is a gift of creation that God has bestowed on all people.

1. Describe how each of the following commands and rules sustains and promotes life.
- Look both ways before you cross the street.
- You shall not lie about your neighbor.
- Stop the car at a red light.

2. Brainstorm a list of additional commands and rules that sustain and promote life. How are these commands and rules gifts to us?

Lutheran Context

1. Martin Luther clearly saw that God's law and commands were connected to God's promises because they show the way in which God, through the resources of wisdom, preserves and sustains all aspects of life. Luther's major contribution to this discussion was his treatment of the Ten Commandments. Luther believed that the Ten Commandments were one of the most important places to gain insights into God's love and mercy in Scripture. He placed them first—in the position of highest importance—in his Catechism, which he saw as a summary of the whole teaching of the Bible.

- Read the Ten Commandments and the explanations of them in *Luther's Small Catechism* (Augsburg Fortress, 2008). Note how Luther begins each explanation with, "We are to fear and love God...." Compare this with Proverbs 1:7.

Bonus Activity:
As a group, come up with a metaphor or image for God's wisdom or law.

Bonus Activity:
Challenge participants to think of other metaphors for the tongue, words, and speech.

Bonus Activity:
Give examples of rules and laws that have not been life-sustaining and life-promoting. You might include laws that led to persecution of the early Christians, slavery in America, and so on. How do we reconcile these rules and laws with God's gift of wisdom to creation?

Bonus Activity:
If you could make one new rule for everyone in your household or neighborhood to follow, what would it be? Why would you choose to make this rule?

Bonus Activity:
Brainstorm some reasons why Luther might have chosen to place the Ten Commandments first in the Small Catechism.

Tip:
Distribute copies of *Luther's Small Catechism* or *Evangelical Lutheran Worship* (see pp. 1160-1161).

SESSION THREE

- Choose one of the commandments and discuss how it shows God's love and mercy.

2. Luther talked about the place of wisdom, law, and commands in his teaching on two kingdoms. We live in these two kingdoms at the same time. In one kingdom, Luther said, God works, through the gospel of forgiveness and promise, to make sure that we understand that we are justified not by what we do, but through God's mercy and grace in the death and resurrection of Jesus Christ. Luther called this the kingdom on the right. In the kingdom on the left (the kingdom of this world or the world of creation), God works through law or commands to preserve and sustain life. God gives the resources of wisdom so that we can sort out or discern the best ways to preserve and care for the lives of our neighbors. This kingdom encompasses all the world's institutions and structures, rules and regulations. Here human insights and wisdom can develop and imagine better ways of living.

- Notice that God is at work in both kingdoms, in different ways. What are some other similarities or differences between the two kingdoms?

Devotional Context

1. "We are justified not by what we do, but through God's mercy and grace in the death and resurrection of Jesus Christ." What do you think about this statement?

2. Tell or write about something in this session or the Bible text that challenges or delights you.

Wrap-up

1. Ask the learners: What did you learn in this session that was new or surprising? How do you see James or your own faith in a different way?

2. If there are any questions to explore further, write them on chart paper or a whiteboard. Ask for volunteers to do further research to share with the group at the next session.

3. Explain and assign any homework for the coming week.

 Bonus Activity: Start or add to a list of signs of God's wisdom in the world.

 Tip: This statement comes directly from the Lutheran Context in the Learner Guide for this session.

 Bonus Activity: Provide a variety of art materials. Invite participants to create something that reminds them of God's gift of wisdom and sustaining care for the world.

 Tip: As in Session 1, some of the category headings you might consider are wisdom, warnings, Christian actions, healthy habits, rich and poor.

Pray

God of all creation, you sustain and care for the world through wisdom and the law. Help us to appreciate these gifts and see you at work in the world. Empower us with your wisdom to care for the world we live in. Amen.

Extending the Conversation (5 minutes)

Homework

1. Read the next session's Scripture text: James 5:7-20.

2. Make a list of rules and commands that you encounter during the next week. Which of these sustain and promote life?

3. Each day, choose one of the Ten Commandments and read through it and Luther's explanation in the Small Catechism.

Enrichment

1. View the movie *Luther* (Eikon Film, 2003) or at least the scenes of Luther being interrogated at the Diet of Worms.

2. Read selections from the book of Proverbs.

Looking Ahead

1. Read the text for the next session: James 5:7-20.

2. Read through the Leader Guide for Session 4 and decide which portions you want to cover in next week's session.

3. Make a checklist of materials you will need to do any of the activities, including Bonus Activities.

SESSION FOUR

James 5:7-20

Leader Session Guide

Focus Statement
Prayer, praise, confession, and healing inspire hope for a community as it waits in the promise of our Lord's return.

Key Verse
Therefore confess your sins to one another, and pray for one another, so that you may be healed. The prayer of the righteous is powerful and effective. James 5:16

Focus Image

© Ikon Images / SuperStock

Wisdom: Healthy Habits that Sustain Christian Hope

Session Preparation

Before You Begin . . .

Take a few moments to think about what inspires you to hope and what sustains your hope.

Session Instructions

1. Read this Leader Session Guide completely and highlight or underline any portions you wish to emphasize with the group. Note any Bonus Activities you wish to do.

2. If you plan to do any special activities, check to see what materials you'll need, if any.

3. Have extra Bibles on hand in case a group member forgets to bring one.

4. Keep in mind that your role is to facilitate the conversation so that everyone has an opportunity to contribute to the discussion.

Session Overview

Early Christians believed that Jesus was returning to earth very soon. James advises readers to be patient and develop healthy habits of prayer, praise, confession, and healing to inspire hope until Jesus comes again.

LITERARY CONTEXT

Throughout the letter, the writer of James offers wisdom and resources for living our lives in this world. The session Scripture text begins with a reference to Jesus' second coming, but it does not go into detail about this event. Early Christians believed that Jesus was coming again soon, but as time passed, people probably became impatient. James responds by encouraging patience and promoting practices that will help believers wait and remain hopeful: prayer, praise, confession, and healing.

HISTORICAL CONTEXT

The writer of James and the original readers of this letter had a strong Jewish heritage. They would have been very familiar with Hebrew Scriptures, including the stories of Job and Elijah. As a result, James does not include background information about these stories. Passing references to Job and Elijah were enough to bring these Old Testament characters into the discussion about patience, suffering, and the power of prayer. Like Job, we can cry out to God in prayers filled with despair, and God will hear us and respond. Like Elijah, we can be patient and persistent in prayer, knowing that God will answer.

Christians throughout the centuries have taken the words of James 5:14-16 to heart by praying for those who are sick and **anointing** their heads with oil. This often includes the laying on of hands as well. Many congregations include prayers for the sick and prayers for healing in worship services. Some congregations offer healing services that include prayers, anointing, and laying on of hands. However your congregation approaches this, it is clear that we are invited and encouraged to pray for those who are sick and ask for healing.

 Anointing:
The pouring of oil on a person's head to set that person apart for leadership (as with the kings of Israel and Judah) or as part of a healing ministry to those who are sick.

Lutheran Context

Martin Luther believed in the power of prayer. His Morning and Evening Blessings, for instance, encouraged believers to start and end every day with prayers of joy and thankfulness for all God has done for us. Like James, Luther also encouraged Christians to forgive, pray, and ask for God's healing with and for one another. He called this reaching out and sharing gifts with one another the "mutual conversation and consolation of the brethren."

The Lutheran church has a history of being committed to healing ministries. For example, the ELCA and Lutheran Church–Missouri Synod have joined with 300 health and human services agencies and organizations to create Lutheran Services in America (LSA). LSA provides a wide range of health-related ministries in the United States and the Caribbean. In fact, 1 in 50 people in the United States receives help from an LSA organization. On a global scale, Lutheran World Federation provides medical and humanitarian aid to people affected by disasters.

Devotional Context

Seeking the restoration of our relationships with God and with one another is a significant part of the life of faith, and confessing our sins and receiving words of forgiveness are important to the life and health of the community of faith. Because of this, most worship services include a time of confession and forgiveness. Confession allows us to recognize the sin in our lives, our inability to wipe away sin on our own, and our need for God's grace through Christ. Forgiveness sets us

SESSION FOUR

free to love and serve God and neighbor. It has the power to heal the brokenness in our lives and relationships.

Be sure to allow time for participants to share stories about times when prayer, praise, confession, or healing strengthened them and inspired hope for the future. You and your group may find that hearing and telling these stories strengthens and inspires your faith and hope.

Facilitator's Prayer

Take a few moments to think about how you have sinned against God and others.

Lord, I confess my sins to you, both known and unknown. By your grace, restore me to a right relationship with you and with others, and help me to forgive as you have forgiven me. Let your Spirit fill me and strengthen me to serve you and share your love with those I meet today. In Jesus' name I pray. Amen.

Tip:
Consider celebrating the completion of your study of James with refreshments or a meal during or at the end of this session.

Gather (10-15 minutes)

Check-in

Welcome each learner to the session. If there are any new participants, consider using name tags again. If possible, refer to learners by name throughout the session. Invite each person to share a highlight or a lowlight from the past week.

Pray

Giver of all good gifts, you give us all we need for today and provide hope for tomorrow. Strengthen us to live in your grace as we wait for Christ's return. Amen.

Focus Activity

Reflect on the Focus Image. What do you think is going on in the illustration? What in life tries your patience? What is worth waiting for? Why?

Open Scripture (10-15 minutes)

Lead the group in reading the text using the *lectio divina* method. (*Lectio divina* is Latin for "holy reading.") This method of Scripture reading may date back as far as the early church.

SESSION FOUR

Before you begin, invite participants to spend a few moments clearing distractions from their minds.

1. *Lectio*: Tell participants to slowly read over the verses to themselves several times, letting the Spirit guide them.

2. *Meditatio*: Ask participants to think about one word or phrase that stands out to them during the reading.

3. *Oratio*: Invite participants to pray silently over the text and the words or phrases they selected.

4. *Contemplatio*: Give participants a few moments to concentrate on God.

Ask for two volunteers from the group—one to read James 5:7-12 and the other to read 5:13-20.

Read James 5:7-20.
- How do you feel as you listen to this text?
- What words or images stand out to you?
- Through this text, what is God calling you to do or to be?

Tip:
If you decide to use the *lectio divina* method of reading Scripture, be sure that everyone has a Bible to use before you begin. Also, be aware that each person may go at a slightly different pace.

Join the Conversation (25-55 minutes)

Literary Context

1. People in the early church believed that Jesus would return to earth very soon. James says, "The coming of the Lord is near" (5:8).
- Read James 5:7-11 and discuss whether the return or second coming of Christ is reason for hope or despair, according to this text.

2. The whole focus of the letter of James and other wisdom writings is on resources for life in this world.
- Read James 5:13-20 and describe how each of these provides help for daily life: prayer, praise, confession, and healing.
- This letter begins and ends with wisdom and the power of prayer (James 1:5-8 and 5:13-20). What might this tell us about the writer? What might it tell us about wisdom and prayer?

Tip:
The early church expected Jesus to come again any day. Today, we still don't know when Jesus will return. However, until he does we have work to do, according to James—caring for those in need, refraining from judging others, praying, praising, being patient, and confessing our sins.

Bonus Activity:
Invite participants to list books and movies about the end of the world or the second coming of Christ. Is the future portrayed with hope or despair?

Bonus Activity:
List other resources for daily life that are described in earlier chapters of James.

Session 4: James 5:7-20

SESSION FOUR

 Bonus Activity:
Read these portions of Job's story: Job 8:1-7; 11:4-6; 15:4-6; and 16:1-22. Note the reasons the friends give for why Job is suffering, the sins they claim he has committed, and Job's responses to them.

 Bonus Activity:
Have participants form two groups to read more about Elijah. Ask the first group to read 1 Kings 17:8-16 and the second group to read 1 Kings 17:17-24. Have groups identify what they learn about Elijah and about God in these texts.

 Bonus Activity:
Have participants react to this quote from Martin Luther: "Even if I knew that tomorrow the world would go to pieces, I would still plant my apple tree." What do they think Luther meant by this statement?

 Bonus Activity:
Invite participants to tell about a time when the friendship and fellowship extended through a community of faith was particularly meaningful to them.

Historical Context

1. The original readers of James were probably very familiar with the story of Job. At the beginning of this Old Testament story, Job loses his property, his children, and his health. Friends come to visit Job and offer explanations for the suffering he is enduring. These explanations provide no comfort to Job, however, and he cries out to God. God answers by reminding Job of the vast universe made by the creator. Job responds, "I know that you can do all things, and that no purpose of yours can be thwarted. . . . I have uttered what I did not understand, things too wonderful for me, which I did not know" (Job 42:2-3). God restores Job's property and health and blesses Job and his wife with more children.

- Review James 5:7-20, especially verse 11. How does knowing something about Job's story help you read and understand this text?

2. The prophet Elijah was also probably very familiar to the original readers of this letter. King Ahab ruled Israel during Elijah's time. Ahab and his wife Jezebel worshiped other gods. Elijah brought the message from God that there would be a drought because of Ahab's sins.

- Read 1 Kings 17:1-7 and 18:41-46. Then review James 5:7-20, especially verses 13-18. How does the account about Elijah and the drought affect your understanding of this text?

Lutheran Context

1. Martin Luther is quoted as saying, "Tomorrow I plan to work, work, from early until late. In fact, I have so much to do that I shall spend the first three hours in prayer." Discuss what you think Luther meant by this. Would the writer of James agree or disagree with Luther on this?

2. Luther taught that one of the most important activities of Christian congregations is the "mutual conversation and consolation of the brethren." We extend friendship and fellowship in Christ as we reach out and share our gifts with one another in the congregation and community. We share the gospel, speak words of forgiveness, pray, and ask for God's healing with and for one another. This is one of the ways God works through us to keep us and sustain us in God's grace and mercy.

SESSION FOUR

- How does James support what Luther taught about mutual conversation and consolation?
- Give examples of how members of your congregation reach out and share their gifts with one another and in your community. How are you involved in this?

Devotional Context

1. As a group, share a time of worship using the prayers in the order for Individual Confession and Forgiveness (*ELW*, pp. 243-244). Read Psalm 103 together as part of this service.

2. James says that prayer, praise, confession, and healing are resources for living each day and inspiring hope in Christ. Tell about a time when one or more of these resources strengthened you and gave you hope for the future.

Wrap-up

1. Ask the learners: What did you learn in this session that was new or surprising? How do you see James or your own faith in a different way?

2. If there are any questions to explore further, write them on chart paper or a whiteboard.

3. Explain and assign any homework for the coming week.

4. Invite participants to reflect on the sessions and what they have learned from the Bible and one another. Invite them to write down strengths, weaknesses, and suggested improvements for the group session. (Make sure participants know that their suggestions are confidential unless they choose to sign their sheets of paper.) Collect these comments at the end of the session.

Pray

Lord, thank you for the gifts of prayer, praise, confession, and healing, which empower us for day-to-day living and inspire us with hope. As we wait for your return, help us to be busy ministering to one another and the world. In your powerful name we pray. Amen.

Tip:
You may want to bring in a church calendar, bulletin, or newsletter to help with this.

Tip:
Distribute copies of *ELW* to participants.

Bonus Activity:
Prayer can help us live each day with hope in Christ, but sometimes prayers seem to go unanswered, or they are answered in ways we do not want or expect. What does this mean?

Tip:
As in Session 1, some of the category headings you might consider are wisdom, warnings, Christian actions, healthy habits, rich and poor.

SESSION FOUR

Extending the Conversation (5 minutes)

Homework

1. Read the entire letter of James in the next week.

2. Consider participating in another Book of Faith adult Bible study.

Enrichment

1. Read the book of Job.

2. View the Wikipedia article "Christian Eschatology" (http://en.wikipedia.org/wiki/Christian_eschatology). Here you'll find descriptions of different positions on Jesus' return.

For Further Reading

The Wounded Healer: Ministry in Contemporary Society by Henri J. M. Nouwen (New York: Doubleday, 1995). Offers suggestions on how to minister to others out of our own woundedness.

When Bad Things Happen to Good People by Harold S. Kushner (New York: Anchor Books, 2004). Provides a Jewish perspective on suffering.

www.ingramcontent.com/pod-product-compliance
Lightning Source LLC
Chambersburg PA
CBHW051427070526
44584CB00023B/3610